ANGOLA

ANGOLA
A PLACE OF CONTRAST

CLAUDIA LETICIA RUÍZ REYES

Copyright © 2012 by Claudia Leticia Ruíz Reyes.

Library of Congress Control Number: 2012907503

ISBN:	Hardcover	978-1-4633-2395-0
	Softcover	978-1-4633-2397-4
	Ebook	978-1-4633-2396-7

All rights reserved. No part of this book may be reproduced or transmitted in any form or by any means, electronic or mechanical, including photocopying, recording, or by any information storage and retrieval system, without permission in writing from the copyright owner.

The views expressed in this work are solely those of the author and do not necessarily reflect the views of the publisher, and the publisher hereby disclaims any responsibility for them.

This book was printed in the United States of America.

To order additional copies of this book, please contact:
Palibrio
1663 Liberty Drive
Suite 200
Bloomington, IN 47403
Tel: 877.407.5847
Fax: +1.812.355.1576
orders@palibrio.com

INDICE

PREAMBLE 9
CULTURAL ROOTS 11
ANGOLAN CULTURE 13
CHALLENGES 15
"INVISIBLE" AND "VISIBLE" 17

I
AN UNCERTAIN FUTURE

I   AN UNCERTAIN FUTURE 23

II
A PLACE CALLED TO BE REBORN

II A COUNTRY CALLED TO BE REBORN 39

THE AWAKENING OF A GIANT 43
CONCLUSIONS 47
DOCUMENTARY SOURCES 49

DEDICATION

This book is the fruit of the disturbing situation of the People from Angola. I thank everyone who is part of this story, particularly those who share the same interest and desire to be the voice of this people. I thank specially, who once told me: closing the door to thought or silencing a person for fear it is like killing that person. Nobody can control every mind; you are free to express your ideas. Most of all, I thank God for the gift of life and the opportunity to share it with our Brothers from Angola. And all the people that in a direct or indirect way made this material possible, thank you. And to you reader, thank you for letting me into your world.

The Author

PREAMBLE

As a Missioner in Angola. When I arrived to this place I had no idea of how the country was, all I knew was that it went through forty years of war. How can you imagine how people are, when they are emerging from the shadows of death and the pain of uncertainty of having a tomorrow? Today it is a growing city as far as structures and urbanization. Here, life is a little agitated so it is important to learn to live with patience and tranquility. It is easy for one to get impatient and to look at life with mistrust. All this is just to let you know some of the story I am about to share with you and about the reality that this country is living today; do not be surprised with what you will read, but rather I invite you to think about your country and what surrounds you. I'll leave this question to you so you reflect on what you are providing to your country; it is not for you to answer it to me, but to the society where you live at. Each nation has its history and it's present. I will share the history and present of the nation where I am sharing my life at.

CULTURAL ROOTS

The cultural patrimony is reflected in the way of living of a population or society. It reveals its history, costumes, traditions, habits, rites, celebrations, gastronomy, architecture, music, and the way of thinking and living, without forgetting about their day by day work. All these elements form what we call the cultural identity of a population. What we are sparks interest and curiosity amongst other people. Our values are projected in our personality and authenticity, with the condition or value of respect for the other.

The cultural identity is without a doubt, a fundamental element of development because by knowing who we are, it makes it easier for us to adapt to changes that the world demands. But it is necessary for development to go hand by hand with our cultural slope. Every attempt of development that ignores cultural identity finds it hard to settle.

ANGOLAN CULTURE

The multifacetic character of the Angolan culture, because of the ethnic and population diversity could be a factor of curiosity to get to know African culture better.

Angola it is a country searching for growth in every level. Angola needs to prove itself. Start from their cultural scope and potentiate their mineral and cultural resources.

CHALLENGES

African traditions have very bad press. Many occidental authors consider it one of the main causes of the sub-development of the African continent. But it is also true that passionate Africans defend and promote their cultural roots. Even though there are groups that call themselves "intellectuals", who attack those traditions. But what means do they provide to help rescue cultural values and to transform these anti-values? "Nobody can play a symphony by themselves, they need an orchestra" (Harfod E. Luccock).

For example, a woman that is considered, not just in theory but in practice also by the traditional African world as a being with the same onthologic value as a man in such a way that we could talk with certainty about the existence of "women rights"? It recognizes and respects the rights of girls and boys? Certain questions of the same kind seem to be out of place, unnecessary matters. We have to do a re-reading of these realities under the light of human rights. Without a "liberation strategy" with respect to traditions, it would experiment a decadence that would make it wabble. However, to considerate the criticism against African traditions as unfounded, would be a lack of honesty and truth. For it makes us see the disparagement of personal freedom, even the lack of humanity in many traditional African practices. I only wish to contribute to an outline of a reading key that could offer a less tragic vision of the traditional World of Africa. Starting mainly from the Bantu culture, of the story of the Angolan people, of the observation and experience of my work.

"INVISIBLE" AND "VISIBLE"

For the bantu cosmology, the notion of the "Universe" refers to the group formed by two spheres, by two different dimensions: the "invisible" and the "visible" (Mbonimpa 1989. Miti, 1991) this bi-dimensionality configures not only the cosmos, the universe, but every being, particularly the human being. The "invisible" prevails and has to prevail over the "visible". We will see what it means invisible and visible, according to the bantu cosmology before indicating the primacy of the "invisible" and of seeing the conferred dignity given to the human person when the same primacy it is applied to the human being scale.

The visible it is everything the world can see throughout life and death. Even though there are some human beings capable of seeing the "invisible" during terrestrial life. Having "double vision". The "invisible" it is the world of spirits, the first of which is God. The "invisible" of the human being is the secret sphere, its interior world, its conscience; the private space reserved for the spirit or spirits that encourage each of us. The spiritual dimension of the human being has to be understood in a serious and profound manner, following the straightness of reason and justice.

Excluding the fetishism and interested interpretations. By the proclamation of the supremacy of the spiritual essence of the human being, the Bantus claim as the incarnation of a spirit, a human being. It is not a thing, meaning that a being destituted of a spirit possesses life. We can also mark out the obligation of treating in a dignified and special manner, all human beings due to their spiritual nature. It has to be respected not just by the community but by each human being as well.

Particular anthropology and ethics we talked about are articulated around a conception of the cosmos, hence of the human being based on a series of principles, three of which we considerate noteworthy: 1st. the primacy of the invisible. 2nd. The imperative unity. 3d. respect towards order.

I

AN UNCERTAIN FUTURE

I

AN UNCERTAIN FUTURE

Hard fight for peace

>Angola was the last Portuguese colony to gain independence. The Angolan people fought for over 14 years against Portuguese colonists. November 11th was marked on Angola's erasable history: it was the day they conquered their independence. The country lived hard moments after a fratricidal war that lasted until the first trimester of 2002. The UNITA, which leader died on February 22nd 2002, became the main factor of human degradation in Angola, taking into hunger and horror millions of civilians around the country.

Of the three nationalist movements that fought for the country's liberation – the Popular Movement for the Liberation of Angola (UNITA) and the National Front for the Liberation of Angola (FNLA) – only the first one was considered by the Organization of African Unity (OUA)

In November of 1964, with the necessary capacity to fight against Portuguese colonialism and assume power over the country. In fact, the MPLA was the first one organized in Angola and the most active movement. The OUA recognized the legitimacy of the government of Agustinho Neto, who declared the independence and assumed the presidency of the country. Same so, the, FNLA and the UNITA initiated a bloody war against the MPLA. Supported by some African countries and by major world powers, those movements justified their actions by stating that they were fighting against the socialist orientations of the MPLA.

Gbadolite was the first piece treaty, after other intents

Foreign soldiers retired from Angola, and Namibia became independent in March of 1990. This fact pointed out the importance that Angola had in the liberation of Namibia and in the fall of the apartheid regime in South Africa. Then negotiations started to solve internal conflicts, initiating with the Franceville Summit, in Gabon on October 1988, followed by the reunion of eight African Chiefs of State in Luanda. Those meetings created conditions for the creation of Gbadolite, in Zaire on June 1989. Besides the meeting and the creation of the Gbadolite Treaties, with Angola's good will and of almost twenty chiefs of African States, the mediation acts of Mobutu Sese Seko, the duality in the conduction of the treaties by the Zaire Dictator whose involvement with the UNITA was notorious, made impossible the compliance of the treaties. In the Bicesse Agreement the Angolan government extended once more their hand to peace. Two years later representatives of the UNITA and of the Angolan government met at Bicesse, Portugal.

Contrary to the Gbadolite meeting, this event ended with an agreement signed by both parts, increasing hope for peace in Angola. It was established a schedule that would end with the first free and democratic elections in Angola, supervised by the United Nations. The government and the UNITA (FAPLA and FALA, respectively) must also dissolve their armies and form a unique one, the Angolan Armed Forces. (FAA).

The newspaper **afrol news** –published this note on the 25th anniversary of the Angolan independence.

Angola celebrated their 25 years of independence, but this date represents also more than 25 years of war between the government of Angola and the UNITA. Since 1998, the conflict has gone through an especially violent phase. Despite that, the government of Angola tries to show to the world that the situation is normal again and that they control more than 90% of the territory.

This speech of normalization is not just given by the government alone. The international community and the United Nations sustain the same speech related to the regained stability. So, the agencies from the United Nations, particularly the World Food Program, will vary the system of general distribution of food to adjust to the "relocation" of people planned by the government. The support from the international community in the form of intensive economical investments (results that are only visible in Luanda and the Atlantic coast) make this normal appearance possible.

The humanitarian organization Medics with No Borders (MSF), present in Angola since 1983, has developed new health and food programs for the population going through the re-initiation of the conflict. These references to "normal" are far from the reality observed by the MSF teams that live and work with the civil population of Angola.

Forced relocations and increase in violence

At the end of 1998, after a few years of relative peace following the treaties in Lusaka, war initiated again in Angola. Since then, the relocated people move in big masses to the cities controlled by the government, while others look for shelter in neighbor countries. These movements of population are produced in waves and each of them marks the episodes of the most violent confrontations between the FAA and UNITA.

This massive movement of relocated people has incremented considerably the population in the cities where the organization is present.

According to the authorities in Angola, the relocated people that are in zones of less government control ran from their homes because of the UNITA. Certainly, it is hard for relocated people to deny this publicly: they talk about escaping from the "enemy" or from the "people in the country side". However, individual stories collected by the MSF in Caala, Kuito and Malange from April to October of 2000, show that taking the party in favor of the government was perceived as the only solution, an election of survival more than an election to join one or the other party, or even to run from them. These massive movements were made in a forced manner, surrounded by an environment of growing violence.

The relocated population not just ran from the fighting zones. They were also utilized and manipulated by both confrontating parties, who wanted to eliminate the people from the zone controlled by the other party or to clean a zone from any enemy presence. Therefore, the relocation of civilians it is utilized as a war strategy. This intention of controlling the population it usually includes punishment acts and retaliation against individuals that remain in zones controlled by the enemy. With each offensive by the government, UNITA relocated and took the whole population with them. It is the only tactic used by UNITA! Every time, we would go to wherever they told us to. In fact, nobody could stay behind because any missing person represented one more person for the government. *Person relocated from the province of Huambo.*

UNITA was going to take the people from my village to "the country" when the FAA arrived. The FAA told us to go with them to Loquembo, and we did. By nightfall, they indicated an area and ordered us to sleep there. Then, UNITA attacked and the FAA fled the scene. UNITA captured me along with 19 men and five women. They tied our arms behind our backs and took us. When we arrived to a bridge over a troubled waters river, they shot at us (not the girls, they took them with them) and threw us into the river with our arms still tied. I was shot on the back and somehow was able to get out of the river. I was the only survivor. I was able to untie myself and ran towards Loquembo. *Person relocated from the province of Malange.*

I was sleeping at home with my family, when at around 4 in the morning 12 men from UNITA came into my house and took me with them. We walked for half an hour. I did not say a thing nor tried to resist. They told me to kneel and to put one hand on a piece of wood on the floor. Three of the men were holding me while a fourth one was hitting me on my forearm with a machete. By the second blow, my forearm fell to the ground. I was told to get up and then they did the same thing with my brother.

The soldiers said: "we do this because the government troops came to Belo Horizonte and you want to join them. Now that we have cut your hands you won't be able to". After them mutilating my brother, they told us: "You can go wherever you want now. Join the MPLA!" Person relocated from the province of *Bié*.

The "troop" (how they usually called the government army) came back to the city and ordered the people to get into the cars if they didn't want to die murdered. We did what they said. There were several families in the "troop's" trucks and we were all taken to Caala.

Person relocated from Huambo.

Elevated mortality rates

The precarious sanitation conditions in the cities, difficulties to get medical attention and food problems have serious repercussions in the health conditions of the population. Various retrospective studies of mortality conducted by the MSF revealed mortality rates superior to the acceptable alert values. A study from the MSF conducted in March of 2000 in Caala revealed elevated mortality rates: 1.68 of each 10,000 people a day in the relocated population, a figure higher than the alert value of 1/10.000/day. The mortality rate in children younger than 5 it is also alarming, with a median of 3.1/10.000/day, a figure higher than the normally accepted one for this age (2). The situation of the resident population is almost the same, especially in children younger than 5, which rate of mortality is 2,13/10.000/day.

A study made by the MSF in Lombe in July of 2000 revealed a mortality rate of 1,4/10.000/day among the general population and of 2,66/10.000/day among children younger than 5 years old.

A research conducted in June of 2000 in Kuito, showed even higher rates among children younger than 5 years old:

4,3/10.000/day in relocated children and 2/10.000/day in resident children. The mortality rate among the adult population was of 1,7/10.000/day.

The elections of 1992 brought hope in the democratic militia

Elections

The government fulfilled its commitments: immobilized great part of the army, of almost 400 thousand men, guaranteed the freedom of the public parties and programmed presidential and legislative elections for September of 1992. During the campaign, which brought an environment of relative peace to the country, the UNITA started showing their real intentions. With a threatening security device they intimidated the population, they started admitting to attacks they denied before, making it clear that they would not accept a result other than their victory.

The elections of 1992 brought hope in the democratic militia. The UNITA did not get what they wanted and the population showed clearly which road they wanted to follow. The MPLA defeated UNITA 54% to 34%

In the legislative elections votes, while for the presidency, José Eduardo dos Santos got 49.6% of the votes, and the UNITA leader got 40,1%. Despite the victory, the agreement stated that if none of the candidates reached a 50% of the votes, there would be another election. But the next round never happened. The UNITA accused of fraudulent elections, against the opinion of the international community, even from the special representative of the general secretary of the United Nations, Margareth Anstee. The leader of the UNITA, retired from the province and ordered to re-start the war at a big scale. The FAPLA have been immobilized, the FAA where still formed, and the FALA where intact. They had two goals: total control of the country, or at least, a big part of it even with the instinct of creating "South Angola".

Popular Resistance

The population of Luanda raised arms to fight the men from Savimbi, who were trying to conquer the capital after the UNITA was surprised by the resistance of the population who, outraged by the violation of the peace treaty, raised arms in several cities and fought against the UNITA forces. In Luanda, the confrontations were brutal and the terrorist forces were expelled from the capital. With time, the same resistance created a progressive growth of murdering groups against civilian population; confrontations on the capital streets were intense and, with the help of the population, the UNITA was expelled.

Various meetings pretending to restart negotiations were made under the patronage of the United Nations.

Namibe, south of Angola, 1992; in Addis Abeba, Ethiopía, between January and March of 1993; and Abidjan, Ivory Coast, in April and May 1993. They all failed due to the intransigence of the UNITA negotiators. After the contacts in Namibe where retaken, the UNITA attacked Uige, in the north of the country. In Addis Abeba, the UNITA abandoned the negotiating table and initiated an attack on Huambo.

In Abidjan, six weeks of negotiations were wasted when the UNITA did not sign an agreement with 38 points, which the Angolan government had already accepted. In this last case, the UNITA demanded that troops from the United Nations get in action while the UNITA and the FAA would get quartered. That was completely against the resolutions of the United Nations which determined, after the elections of 1992, the retreat of the UNITA troops from the occupied territories. The war was escalating even more.

Lusaka

Lusaka was the third great summit mediated by the United Nations in the search for peace on November the 20th 1994, after months of hard negotiations, the minister of Foreign Affairs of Angola Venancio de Moura, and the general secretary of UNITA, Manuvakola, signed the Protocol of Lusaka in Zambia, which resumed the basic points of the Bicesse Agreement.

They hoped that this new agreement would bring definitive peace due to several good reasons: the Cold War was over, and the world was starting to incline more towards defending human rights. And mostly because in May of 1993 the United States of America, represented by the figure of Bill Clinton, finally recognized the Angolan Government. More than repairing the injustice of its predecessors, the north american president had the goal of diminishing any political connotation in the terrorist attacks of the UNITA. Among other things, the Protocol of Lusaka anticipated the creation of a government of national reconciliation, reaffirmed the immobilization of military forces from both sides and the delivery to government authorities of the areas controlled by the UNITA. Despite the efforts of the United Nations, again nothing worked as planned, even the immobilization of troops. The FAA reduced their troops to 70 thousand men, but the UNITA continued reluctant to integrate their man into the unique armed forces.

**Savimbi and his men continued ignoring
the peace treaties and the Government of Reconciliation**

Government of Reconciliation

In the intent to overcome the successive impasses from the UNITA in the search for peace, president José Eduardo dos Santos decided to start, on April of 1997, the National Government of Reconciliation and Unity (GURN), which should've practiced starting after the delivery of territories occupied by the revels. So, the UNITA integrated various ministries and occupied 70 places in the National Council, which were empty since the interruption of the electoral process in 1992. During this process, the UNITA wouldn't give up on their terrorism. In December of 1995, attacked Soyo, where the main American and French oil branches are located.

In March of 1998, their forces promoted the massacre of more than 200 civilians in the province of Malanje. The terrorist movement continued training their troops; this was verified on August of 1997 by the peace force of the Mission of the United Nations in Angola (MONUA).

The proof of it came in the same year, through the general secretary of UNITA, Eugénio Manuvakola, who disappeared after the Protocol of Lusaka was signed. He ran from Bailundo, general headquarters of Huambo. Manuvakola revealed that he has been apprehended and tortured for signing the agreement without anticipating the delivery of the provinces of Huambo, Bié and Benguela to the UNITA. He revealed also that the UNITA forces were getting re-organized to initiate the war again. At this point, the MONUA failed in seeing that the leader of the revels took advantage of the halt to the fire to smuggle diamonds and with the money obtained, he strengthen his army with sophisticated weapons and Ukrainian mercenaries, Tutsis and south Africans. Meanwhile, the Angolan government tried to return to the negotiation tables and make concessions. The war continued until the rebel leader died in combat on February 22nd of 2002. After almost 40 years of conflict, 5 of every 6 Angolans never knew peace. Numbers are unknown, but casualties rise to more than a million. Almost 4 million people, a third of the population, are war dislocated, and were obligated to leave their homes.

Angola, which has one of the biggest diamond reservoirs in the planet and with a production of 800 thousand barrels of oil per day, was not able to enjoy such wealth and give better living conditions to its population due to the criminal actions of the guerrilla. The country is in the 161st place worldwide in the ranking of Human development Index.

Peace reaches Angola

With the death of the leader of the guerrilla, they initiated exploratory contacts in Luena, Moxico, between the residual forces of the UNITA and the FAA, process that culminated with the signature of a Protocol of Understanding between both parts on April 4th 2002. On the 29th of the same month and year, it was signed in Luanda, the document that would end the war in Angola and opened the doors of reconstruction of the country, the reconciliation of those who, in the past, would only know how to live in war. The historical hug between the President José Eduardo dos Santos and the General of UNITA Kamorteiro. The confinement of the UNITA troops, the absorption of them to the national army, the resettlement of the dislocated population to their places of origin, as well as the social framework of the old revels, were the main deeds that the Angolan government prioritized, along with the reconstruction of the economical and social infrastructures destroyed during the war. These deeds, due to their amplitude, demanded a big effort from all the Angolan people, as well as the contest of the international community, given the bulked amounts of money asked. So, in times of peace, the fight of the Angolan people is to reconstruct the country economically and socially; to get Angola to the place they deserve in Africa and in the world.

II

A PLACE CALLED TO BE REBORN

II

A COUNTRY CALLED TO BE REBORN

The fire has stopped, but Angola has no peace just yet. The pain of the less fortunate is still there. We, foreign visitors always get a recommendation when allowed to enter the country, <*It is not allowed to take photographs, use binoculars or any GPS equipment near government buildings, military or security installations. It proceeds to the surveillance by street cameras to inspect the relevant technical ban.*>. Fear to what? Why so many restrictions? I was asking on my arrival to the country, isn't the country in peace?

People from Angola ask for justice and equity, dream with a better way of living, but, how can they recuperate what they lost? How can they do it if they do not have whats considered basic needs? The parameters between rich and poor are enormous. How can they heal their wounds in an unequal world on which psychiatric hospitals do not have space for one more patient because they are full? Where the people die young due to a lack of medical attention or because it is too precarious.

There are private clinics but they are very expensive. Where is the money from the reaches from the subsoil of this country? This is what they call liberty? Were the one that declares itself in favor of human rights is scared and silenced because of the interests of a few that are over human dignity? My person is put on the Fletcher by being the voice of the history of these people. In many occasions I've asked myself: where does peace begin, where are human rights located?

Through the continuous growth of the Nation's wealth, the "Angolan Paradox" got worse, of being a rich country with a very poor population. Poverty it is a crucial challenge for public politics in the coming years, also a reason for mobilization of various social authors. It is not enough to create modern structures, a better organization of the community is also needed. By 2012, elections in this country are expected, we will see if Angola will take a testimony step for democracy, so needed by the African Continent.

Motivated by the spirit

Exclusion creates degradation of the human being, stimulates marginalization, divides the world between the ones participating of the scientific and technological development events, enjoying the advantages of consuming, and those that have nothing, that hide and feel relegated from the great avenues of the world. This added to a cultural crisis and to the economical development in which many have lost the will of living with optimism and hope. It is necessary to retake the values that have been drowned by war. The base is happiness, family, community, and sharing life. It is time to be reborn looking at the present and the future with optimism, cultivating a positive spirit without leaving reality. Optimism is not the contrary of acceptance of real problems or with negative aspects of an unhappy situation; but taken with tranquility and patience, strategies can be created that could help solve the problems in the best way possible. To maintain a state of "positive spirit", helps us stay always in check of others needs. It is proven that and optimistic spirit, stimulates nice memories by blocking the unhappy ones. On the contrary, people that feel sad tend to have negative experiences or to forget the nice ones. The best method to stimulate positive thinking is by adopting a positive thinking style. Even when the road seems so hard that makes us feel emptiness in our stomach, to change that dark cloud we need to own our decisions. We need to believe on a better future, and this will take people to betting everything to make this country prosperous and pacific. Because peace initiates in the heart of each human being, and the prosperity of the efforts of each one.

THE AWAKENING OF A GIANT

ANGOLA
I want to live in perpetual peace. I want to see reconciled and active people in the socio-economic and cultural development of the country.

ANGOLA
I want to see your children run freely throughout the territory, to consolidate fraternity ties.

ANGOLA
I want to be a privileged world touristic destination. So visitors can admire its unparalleled beauty

ANGOLA
I want to continue being a homely country, by guaranteeing security.

ANGOLA
I want to be a country opened to big debates, which values its traditions and rich cultures.

ANGOLA, I want to be equal to you, dynamic, irradiating to the world a message of hope, progress, fraternity and openness.

ANGOLA
Is and always will be of all the different Angolan tribes, creeds and political options living in harmony and working together for the common good of this society.

ANGOLA deserves all the love from the Angolan people and the support of the international community.

"canata"

ANGOLA IT IS CALLED TO CREATE A NEW LIFE FOR THE NEXT GENERATIONS

CONCLUSIONS

These pages are based on the history of the Angolan people. From its cultural roots, its fight for liberty and actual reality. My wish is to help awake the responsibility awareness that all human beings have in the decision of the road to walk of a Nation. We are all participants; we are all important actors in the process of change.

I hope that every reader finds in these pages encouragement to transcend, by taking conscience of their role in the construction of society, living day by day with hope and happiness. I invite you to bet everything for the common good and to overcome the chains of selfishness in this world that lives in intolerance and desperation. Let's be accomplices in the belief that this is possible.

DOCUMENTARY SOURCES

- NUNSE, D,A SURVERY REPORT FOR THE BANTU LENGUAGES,HTP//WWWW.SIT.ORG/SILESR/2002/SILERSR2002-016.HTM
- JORNAL DE ANGOLA
- REPORTS FROM THE UNITED NATIONS IN THE PROCESS OF PEACE
- AMNESTY INTERNATIONAL REPORT
- FOLHA 8 DE ANGOLA
- WWW.UNICEF.ORG.
- AFROL NEWS
- TESTIMONY OF PEOPLE WHO'S IDENTITY WAS KEPT CONFIDENTIAL TO PROTECT THEIR SECURITY.